DISNEY GRAVITY FALLS MAD LIBS

by Laura M

Mad
An Imprint of Penguin Random House

MAD LIBS
Penguin Young Readers Group
An Imprint of Penguin Random House LLC

Mad Libs format copyright © 2018 by Penguin Random House LLC. All rights reserved.

Concept created by Roger Price & Leonard Stern

Based on the series created by Alex Hirsch

Copyright © 2018 Disney Enterprises, Inc. All rights reserved.

Published by Mad Libs,
an imprint of Penguin Random House LLC,
345 Hudson Street, New York, New York 10014.
Printed in the USA.

ISBN 9781524787134
3 5 7 9 10 8 6 4 2

MAD LIBS® is a game for people who don't like games! It can be played by one, two, three, four, or forty.

● RIDICULOUSLY SIMPLE DIRECTIONS

In this tablet you will find stories containing blank spaces where words are left out. One player, the READER, selects one of these stories. The READER does not tell anyone what the story is about. Instead, he/she asks the other players, the WRITERS, to give him/her words. These words are used to fill in the blank spaces in the story.

● TO PLAY

The READER asks each WRITER in turn to call out a word—an adjective or a noun or whatever the space calls for—and uses them to fill in the blank spaces in the story. The result is a MAD LIBS® game.

When the READER then reads the completed MAD LIBS® game to the other players, they will discover that they have written a story that is fantastic, screamingly funny, shocking, silly, crazy, or just plain dumb—depending upon which words each WRITER called out.

● EXAMPLE (*Before* and *After*)

" _____ !" he said _____
        EXCLAMATION   ADVERB

as he jumped into his convertible _____ and
                                                              NOUN

drove off with his _____ wife.
                              ADJECTIVE

" _____**OUCH**_____ !" he said _____**STUPIDLY**_____
        EXCLAMATION   ADVERB

as he jumped into his convertible _____**CAT**_____ and
                                                              NOUN

drove off with his _____**BRAVE**_____ wife.
                              ADJECTIVE

MAD LIBS
QUICK REVIEW

In case you have forgotten what adjectives, adverbs, nouns, and verbs are, here is a quick review:

An ADJECTIVE describes something or somebody. *Lumpy*, *soft*, *ugly*, *messy*, and *short* are adjectives.

An ADVERB tells how something is done. It modifies a verb and usually ends in "ly." *Modestly*, *stupidly*, *greedily*, and *carefully* are adverbs.

A NOUN is the name of a person, place, or thing. *Sidewalk*, *umbrella*, *bridle*, *bathtub*, and *nose* are nouns.

A VERB is an action word. *Run*, *pitch*, *jump*, and *swim* are verbs. Put the verbs in past tense if the directions say PAST TENSE. *Ran*, *pitched*, *jumped*, and *swam* are verbs in the past tense.

When we ask for A PLACE, we mean any sort of place: a country or city (*Spain*, *Cleveland*) or a room (*bathroom*, *kitchen*).

An EXCLAMATION or SILLY WORD is any sort of funny sound, gasp, grunt, or outcry, like *Wow!*, *Ouch!*, *Whomp!*, *Ick!*, and *Gadzooks!*

When we ask for specific words, like a NUMBER, a COLOR, an ANIMAL, or a PART OF THE BODY, we mean a word that is one of those things, like *seven*, *blue*, *horse*, or *head*.

When we ask for a PLURAL, it means more than one. For example, *cat* pluralized is *cats*.

MAD LIBS® is fun to play with friends, but you can also play it by yourself! To begin with, DO NOT look at the story on the page below. Fill in the blanks on this page with the words called for. Then, using the words you have selected, fill in the blank spaces in the story.

Now you've created your own hilarious MAD LIBS® game!

NOW ENTERING GRAVITY FALLS

PLURAL NOUN _____

NOUN _____

ADJECTIVE _____

ADJECTIVE _____

ADJECTIVE _____

PLURAL NOUN _____

VERB ENDING IN "ING" _____

ADJECTIVE _____

PLURAL NOUN _____

ADJECTIVE _____

PART OF THE BODY _____

PLURAL NOUN _____

Dipper: Ah, summer. Nothing beats heading into the great outdoors

for some ___aliens___. It all started when my parents sent me and
<u>PLURAL NOUN</u>

my twin ___UFO___, Mabel, up to Gravity Falls, Oregon, to
<u>NOUN</u>

spend the summer with our ___poop trail___-uncle, Stan.
<u>ADJECTIVE</u>

Mabel: He's this weird, ___secretive___, old man who lives in a
<u>ADJECTIVE</u>

tourist trap called the Mystery Shack!

Dipper: The real mystery is why anyone goes to that ___wealthy___
<u>ADJECTIVE</u>

dump. Most of the ___Bears___ are fake!
<u>PLURAL NOUN</u>

Mabel: But the Shack's got a gift shop and even a/an ___singing___
<u>VERB ENDING IN "ING"</u>

machine! When we first came to Gravity Falls, I knew we were gonna

have a/an ___sharp___ time!
<u>ADJECTIVE</u>

Dipper: I couldn't wait to solve some ___Trees___ with the
<u>PLURAL NOUN</u>

journal I found. Who is the author? Why is Gravity Falls such a/an

___pretty___ place? Why does Mabel think that bedazzling her
<u>ADJECTIVE</u>

___belly___ is a good idea?
<u>PART OF THE BODY</u>

Mabel: So . . . sparkly . . .

Dipper: Maybe some ___cubing___ are better left unsolved . . .
<u>PLURAL NOUN</u>

MAD LIBS® is fun to play with friends, but you can also play it by yourself! To begin with, DO NOT look at the story on the page below. Fill in the blanks on this page with the words called for. Then, using the words you have selected, fill in the blank spaces in the story.

Now you've created your own hilarious MAD LIBS® game!

WELCOME TO THE MYSTERY SHACK

NOUN _____

NOUN _____

ADJECTIVE _____

EXCLAMATION _____

PLURAL NOUN _____

VERB _____

NOUN _____

VERB ENDING IN "ING" _____

PART OF THE BODY _____

NOUN _____

NOUN _____

ADJECTIVE _____

CELEBRITY (MALE) _____

PERSON IN ROOM _____

PLURAL NOUN _____

PLURAL NOUN _____

NOUN _____

MAD LIBS®
WELCOME TO THE
MYSTERY SHACK

Hey, dudes! It's your friendly, neighborhood handy-__girl__,
                                                   NOUN

Soos. I'm here to welcome you to—__eyeball__-roll, please—the
                                   NOUN

__creepy__ Shack! __Hot Belgium Waffles__, this place has all kinds of
ADJECTIVE   EXCLAMATION

kooky __ducks__ to __jump__ at, like an invisible
       PLURAL NOUN   VERB

__shack__, __running__ saucers, the __toe__
  NOUN   VERB ENDING IN "ING"   PART OF THE BODY

of a T. rex, and that's just the tip of the __DeDemore D__, dudes! This
                                              NOUN

one time, I even found a secret __beach__, and hidden behind it
                                 NOUN

was this __alert__ wax-figure museum. There was one wax
          ADJECTIVE

figure that looked like __The Rock__, and I thought it was
                         CELEBRITY (MALE)

funny because __Steve__ has a crush on him. But then, it
               PERSON IN ROOM

wasn't funny because those wax __people__ tried to kill me.
                                PLURAL NOUN

Man, what a great job! Whether I'm fixin' up the __trees__ or
                                                  PLURAL NOUN

cleaning out Mr. Pines's clogged __horse__, it's always a magical
                                  NOUN

time at the Mystery Shack!

MAD LIBS® is fun to play with friends, but you can also play it by yourself! To begin with, DO NOT look at the story on the page below. Fill in the blanks on this page with the words called for. Then, using the words you have selected, fill in the blank spaces in the story.

Now you've created your own hilarious MAD LIBS® game!

MYSTERY SHACK TV COMMERCIAL

VERB ENDING IN "ING" _____

ADJECTIVE _____

NUMBER _____

SILLY WORD _____

NOUN _____

NOUN _____

PART OF THE BODY _____

NUMBER _____

NOUN _____

PERSON IN ROOM _____

ADJECTIVE _____

NOUN _____

PLURAL NOUN _____

NOUN _____

ADJECTIVE _____

NOUN _____

MAD LIBS®
MYSTERY SHACK
TV COMMERCIAL

Stan: Is the camera _____, Soos?
_{VERB ENDING IN "ING"}

Soos: Rolling, Mr. Pines!

Dipper: Okay! _____ Shack TV commercial, take
_{ADJECTIVE}

_____. And, action!
_{NUMBER}

Stan: Hi, I'm Mr. Mystery. Come on down to . . . _____!
_{SILLY WORD}

Uh, what's my _____?
_{NOUN}

Dipper: Your line is, "Come on down to the Mystery _____!"
_{NOUN}

Stan: Right! Right! Doesn't really roll off the _____, does it?
_{PART OF THE BODY}

Dipper: Uh, sure. Mystery Shack TV commercial, take

_____. And, _____!
_{NUMBER}   _{NOUN}

Stan: Hi, I'm Mr. _____. Come on down to the
_{PERSON IN ROOM}

_____ _____! Where you won't believe your
_{ADJECTIVE}   _{NOUN}

_____!
_{PLURAL NOUN}

Dipper: Close enough! That's a/an _____, everybody!
_{NOUN}

Stan: Wow! That last take felt _____!
_{ADJECTIVE}

Soos: Hey, dudes? One problem. I just realized I left the _____
_{NOUN}

cap on the camera!

From GRAVITY FALLS MAD LIBS® • Copyright © 2018 Disney Enterprises, Inc. All rights reserved.
Published by Mad Libs, an imprint of Penguin Random House LLC.

MAD LIBS® is fun to play with friends, but you can also play it by yourself! To begin with, DO NOT look at the story on the page below. Fill in the blanks on this page with the words called for. Then, using the words you have selected, fill in the blank spaces in the story.

Now you've created your own hilarious MAD LIBS® game!

MABEL'S GUIDE TO DATING!

NOUN _____

ADJECTIVE _____

PLURAL NOUN _____

VERB ENDING IN "ING" _____

TYPE OF FOOD _____

NOUN _____

VERB ENDING IN "ING" _____

PLURAL NOUN _____

VERB _____

NOUN _____

NOUN _____

ADJECTIVE _____

NOUN _____

NOUN _____

ARTICLE OF CLOTHING _____

MAD LIBS®

MABEL'S GUIDE TO DATING!

Guess what? It's Mabel! When it comes to boys, I'm kind of a big

_____. That's why I'm here to help you feel more
    NOUN

_____ in the dating world! Here are _____ to make
    ADJECTIVE   PLURAL NOUN

_____ easy-peasy-_____-squeezy!
   VERB ENDING IN "ING"   TYPE OF FOOD

1. Before I had my first romantic _____ with Mermando, I
                             NOUN

had to free him from the local _____ pool. So, if your
                        VERB ENDING IN "ING"

boyfriend wants to go home to his family of mer-_____,
                                  PLURAL NOUN

help him out! He'll _____ you for it later!
             VERB

2. If someone you don't like wants to go out on a/an _____—
                             NOUN

cough, Gideon, cough—honesty is the best _____!
                               NOUN

Otherwise, you might set off his _____ evil side!
                        ADJECTIVE

3. If your boy-_____ tells you he has a secret _____,
          NOUN   NOUN

don't be too disappointed if it turns out that he's just a pile of gnomes

in a/an _____.
   ARTICLE OF CLOTHING

MAD LIBS® is fun to play with friends, but you can also play it by yourself! To begin with, DO NOT look at the story on the page below. Fill in the blanks on this page with the words called for. Then, using the words you have selected, fill in the blank spaces in the story.

Now you've created your own hilarious MAD LIBS® game!

JOURNAL ENTRY: GNOMES

EXCLAMATION _____

ADJECTIVE _____

NOUN _____

NOUN _____

PLURAL NOUN _____

A PLACE _____

ADVERB _____

VEHICLE (PLURAL) _____

NUMBER _____

SILLY WORD _____

ADJECTIVE _____

PLURAL NOUN _____

PART OF THE BODY _____

NOUN _____

ADJECTIVE _____

PLURAL NOUN _____

MAD LIBS

JOURNAL ENTRY: GNOMES

Dipper here! _____, what a/an _____ day. A
                  EXCLAMATION   ADJECTIVE

creepy group of gnomes posing as a/an _____ kidnapped
                                          NOUN

Mabel and tried to crown her _____ of their kingdom! First,
                                   NOUN

the _____ carried Mabel deep into (the) _____.
       PLURAL NOUN   A PLACE

_____, I was able to find them. Then, Mabel and I escaped
   ADVERB

in one of Stan's golf _____. After racing away for a minute
                      VEHICLE (PLURAL)

or _____, we thought we were in the clear. That's when we
      NUMBER

heard a loud "_____" coming from behind us. We were
                SILLY WORD

being chased by what appeared to be a/an _____ gnome
                                              ADJECTIVE

giant! Then, Mabel discovered the gnomes' ultimate weakness—

_____! She single-_____-edly solved a mystery
  PLURAL NOUN   PART OF THE BODY

even the author of this mysterious _____ couldn't solve! All
                                        NOUN

I have to do now is write her _____ discovery down in the
                                  ADJECTIVE

gnomes' journal entry . . . there we go! Filling in the _____
                                                         PLURAL NOUN

is pretty fun, right?

MAD LIBS® is fun to play with friends, but you can also play it by yourself! To begin with, DO NOT look at the story on the page below. Fill in the blanks on this page with the words called for. Then, using the words you have selected, fill in the blank spaces in the story.

Now you've created your own hilarious MAD LIBS® game!

ON BREAK AT THE MYSTERY SHACK (WITH WENDY!)

ANIMAL (PLURAL) _____

VERB ENDING IN "ING" _____

PLURAL NOUN _____

SAME PLURAL NOUN _____

VERB _____

PART OF THE BODY _____

ADJECTIVE _____

PLURAL NOUN _____

NOUN _____

ADJECTIVE _____

NOUN _____

VERB _____

ADJECTIVE _____

PLURAL NOUN _____

PLURAL NOUN _____

MAD LIBS
ON BREAK AT THE MYSTERY SHACK (WITH WENDY!)

Whaddup, _____! Let me level with you—
ANIMAL (PLURAL)

_____ at the Mystery Shack stinks, okay? The exhibits
VERB ENDING IN "ING"

smell like _____, Stan smells like _____ . . .
PLURAL NOUN   SAME PLURAL NOUN

but, if you're stuck working here for the summer, don't _____!
VERB

Wendy's got your _____. Here are some _____
PART OF THE BODY   ADJECTIVE

ways to goof off during your break:

1. Invite your _____: If your friends show up during your
PLURAL NOUN

shift, it'll go by a lot faster. Just try to be sly if your ex-_____
NOUN

wants to come by . . . ugh, Robbie is so _____!
ADJECTIVE

2. Dance-offs: Mabel's usually got a boom _____ on hand,
NOUN

so _____ up that music and see who's got the most
VERB

_____ moves! Again, Stan not being around is key here.
ADJECTIVE

3. Drag racing: What's that, Stan? The go-karts are for moving the

_____ around only? Sorry, didn't hear you over me and
PLURAL NOUN

Dipper revving up the _____!
PLURAL NOUN

MAD LIBS® is fun to play with friends, but you can also play it by yourself! To begin with, DO NOT look at the story on the page below. Fill in the blanks on this page with the words called for. Then, using the words you have selected, fill in the blank spaces in the story.

Now you've created your own hilarious MAD LIBS® game!

HAPPY SUMMERWEEN!

PLURAL NOUN _____

NUMBER _____

ADJECTIVE _____

NOUN _____

ADJECTIVE _____

VERB _____

NOUN _____

A PLACE _____

PERSON IN ROOM _____

ADJECTIVE _____

VERB ENDING IN "ING" _____

ADJECTIVE _____

TYPE OF FOOD (PLURAL) _____

NOUN _____

NUMBER _____

NOUN _____

MAD LIBS
HAPPY SUMMERWEEN!

Did you know that the _____ of Gravity Falls celebrate

PLURAL NOUN

Halloween _____ times a year? Once in October (you know,

NUMBER

the _____ way) and again in the heat of _____.

ADJECTIVE   NOUN

Dipper and Mabel's Summerween was _____, to say the

ADJECTIVE

least! After all, a/an _____-in with the Summerween Trickster

VERB

is no _____! Here's how to enjoy Summerween:

NOUN

- If you're going to (the) _____ to pick up some

A PLACE

  Summerween goodies and costumes, maybe leave Grunkle

  _____ at home. Old _____-skates and

PERSON IN ROOM   ADJECTIVE

  honest retailers don't really mix.

- Go trick-or-_____! Even if someone really

VERB ENDING IN "ING"

  _____, like Wendy, invites you to a party instead,

ADJECTIVE

  you'll likely have a better time pounding the pavement in search

  of chocolate _____.

TYPE OF FOOD (PLURAL)

- Keep Soos away from cheesy _____-ween decorations.

NOUN

  He's usually helpful in a jam, but is as useful as a/an

  _____-legged _____ when he's distracted!

NUMBER   NOUN

MAD LIBS® is fun to play with friends, but you can also play it by yourself! To begin with, DO NOT look at the story on the page below. Fill in the blanks on this page with the words called for. Then, using the words you have selected, fill in the blank spaces in the story.

Now you've created your own hilarious MAD LIBS® game!

MABEL'S GUIDE TO PET PIGS!

ANIMAL (PLURAL) _____

ADJECTIVE _____

PART OF THE BODY (PLURAL) _____

ADJECTIVE _____

VERB ENDING IN "ING" _____

TYPE OF LIQUID _____

TYPE OF FOOD (PLURAL) _____

ADJECTIVE _____

NOUN _____

CELEBRITY _____

NOUN _____

ADJECTIVE _____

TYPE OF FOOD (PLURAL) _____

ARTICLE OF CLOTHING (PLURAL) _____

ADJECTIVE _____

MAD LIBS

MABEL'S GUIDE TO PET PIGS!

Take it from me and Waddles—_____ are cute, very
                                 ANIMAL (PLURAL)

cute, and (my final point) pigs are really, really _____! Just
                                                   ADJECTIVE

look at their curly, little _____! Here are some
                            PART OF THE BODY (PLURAL)

pointers on how to be the most _____ pig parent ever!
                                ADJECTIVE

1. Sharing is _____! So if you've got a/an
              VERB ENDING IN "ING"

_____-shake or any _____, it'll taste even
TYPE OF LIQUID   TYPE OF FOOD (PLURAL)

better if you share it with your pig! Try it. I promise it's not

_____!
ADJECTIVE

2. Dance parties are just as important to a pig as food and

_____! When it's just Waddles and _____ in
NOUN   CELEBRITY

the Mystery _____, we like to break out some
            NOUN

_____ '80s pop music and go _____!
ADJECTIVE   TYPE OF FOOD (PLURAL)

3. Make sure you knit matching _____ for you
                                ARTICLE OF CLOTHING (PLURAL)

and your piggy pal. Pigs like to feel _____, too!
                                      ADJECTIVE

MAD LIBS® is fun to play with friends, but you can also play it by yourself! To begin with, DO NOT look at the story on the page below. Fill in the blanks on this page with the words called for. Then, using the words you have selected, fill in the blank spaces in the story.

Now you've created your own hilarious MAD LIBS® game!

JOURNAL ENTRY: THE UNDEAD

EXCLAMATION _____

VERB ENDING IN "ING" _____

OCCUPATION (PLURAL) _____

ADJECTIVE _____

PLURAL NOUN _____

ADJECTIVE _____

ADVERB _____

NOUN _____

VERB ENDING IN "ING" _____

PART OF THE BODY _____

NOUN _____

ADJECTIVE _____

NOUN _____

ADJECTIVE _____

NOUN _____

NOUN _____

MAD LIBS
JOURNAL ENTRY:
THE UNDEAD

It's Dipper again! _____, you won't believe what happened
<u>EXCLAMATION</u>

tonight at the grand re-_____ of the Mystery Shack.
<u>VERB ENDING IN "ING"</u>

After a pair of government _____ showed up to
<u>OCCUPATION (PLURAL)</u>

question Stan about _____ activity in town, I volunteered to
<u>ADJECTIVE</u>

help search for paranormal _____. _____ story
<u>PLURAL NOUN</u> <u>ADJECTIVE</u>

short, I _____ unleashed a ton of zombies. Poor Soos got
<u>ADVERB</u>

bitten and turned into a/an _____ himself! The zombies
<u>NOUN</u>

and Soos soon had me and Mabel _____ for our lives!
<u>VERB ENDING IN "ING"</u>

Suddenly, Grunkle Stan showed up and started to kick some zombie

_____! He was fighting zombies like it was nobody's
<u>PART OF THE BODY</u>

_____. Thanks to some _____ messages written
<u>NOUN</u> <u>ADJECTIVE</u>

in invisible _____ in this journal, the three of us managed to
<u>NOUN</u>

defeat the zombies and cure _____ Soos. Okay, okay, Mabel's
<u>ADJECTIVE</u>

karaoke _____ was a big help, too. For the record, I still
<u>NOUN</u>

haven't signed off on the band name _____ Patrol Alpha!
<u>NOUN</u>

MAD LIBS® is fun to play with friends, but you can also play it by yourself! To begin with, DO NOT look at the story on the page below. Fill in the blanks on this page with the words called for. Then, using the words you have selected, fill in the blank spaces in the story.

Now you've created your own hilarious MAD LIBS® game!

MR. MYSTERY'S
WORDS OF WISDOM

ADJECTIVE _____

OCCUPATION (PLURAL) _____

PLURAL NOUN _____

PLURAL NOUN _____

NOUN _____

ADJECTIVE _____

NOUN _____

PLURAL NOUN _____

NOUN _____

ADJECTIVE _____

CELEBRITY (MALE) _____

ADJECTIVE _____

PART OF THE BODY _____

NOUN _____

PERSON IN ROOM _____

ADJECTIVE _____

MAD LIBS
MR. MYSTERY'S
WORDS OF WISDOM

Ladies and _____-men, are you tired of greedy con
_____ADJECTIVE_____

_____ stealing your hard-earned _____?
OCCUPATION (PLURAL)   PLURAL NOUN

Do you want to experience the real _____ of Gravity Falls,
                                        PLURAL NOUN

instead of getting ripped off by some bratty _____ with a
                                                  NOUN

fake name? Well, listen up, 'cause Mr. Mystery's got some

_____ advice for you: Stay away from Li'l Gideon's
      ADJECTIVE

_____ o' Telepathy at all _____! Spend your
    NOUN   PLURAL NOUN

vacation with a stand-up _____ like me, not with a/an
                              NOUN

_____, snot-nosed kid with hair like some quack
    ADJECTIVE

_____ impersonator! All his so-called _____
CELEBRITY (MALE)   ADJECTIVE

abilities are bogus! And if you really think Gideon can read your

_____, you've got another _____ comin'! So
PART OF THE BODY   NOUN

forget about Li'l _____, and come on down to the Mystery
                  PERSON IN ROOM

Shack! It's where the _____ magic happens!
                          ADJECTIVE

MAD LIBS® is fun to play with friends, but you can also play it by yourself! To begin with, DO NOT look at the story on the page below. Fill in the blanks on this page with the words called for. Then, using the words you have selected, fill in the blank spaces in the story.

Now you've created your own hilarious MAD LIBS® game!

WELL, WELL, WELL

ADJECTIVE _____

PLURAL NOUN _____

PLURAL NOUN _____

VERB _____

PLURAL NOUN _____

PART OF THE BODY _____

ADJECTIVE _____

PLURAL NOUN _____

EXCLAMATION _____

TYPE OF LIQUID _____

PART OF THE BODY (PLURAL) _____

NOUN _____

NOUN _____

PLURAL NOUN _____

MAD◉LIBS®

WELL, WELL, WELL

NAME'S BILL CIPHER! YOU MIGHT REMEMBER ME AS THE

_____, INTERDIMENSIONAL DEMON FROM YOUR
ADJECTIVE

DARKEST _____. FANCY SEEING ME HERE, RIGHT?
PLURAL NOUN

FILLING IN THE BLANKS MIGHT BE ALL FUN AND

_____ NOW, BUT JUST YOU _____. IT'S
PLURAL NOUN _VERB_

ABOUT TO GET A WHOLE LOT DARKER FROM HERE ON

OUT. YOU WON'T BELIEVE THE _____ YOU'RE
PLURAL NOUN

ABOUT TO UNCOVER ABOUT GRAVITY FALLS. SOME OF

THEM ARE REAL _____-TEASERS, WHILE
PART OF THE BODY

OTHERS ARE JUST PLAIN _____. HILARIOUS,
ADJECTIVE

RIGHT? YOU HUMANS AND YOUR SILLY _____.
PLURAL NOUN

_____, IF I WERE HUMAN, I'D PUT EMOTIONS
EXCLAMATION

ASIDE AND FOCUS ON THE FUN STUFF—LIKE POURING

_____ INTO MY OWN _____!
TYPE OF LIQUID _PART OF THE BODY (PLURAL)_

BUT I DIGRESS. JUST REMEMBER—REALITY IS A/AN

_____, THE UNIVERSE IS A/AN _____, BUY
NOUN _NOUN_

_____. BYEEEEEE!!!
PLURAL NOUN

MAD LIBS® is fun to play with friends, but you can also play it by yourself! To begin with, DO NOT look at the story on the page below. Fill in the blanks on this page with the words called for. Then, using the words you have selected, fill in the blank spaces in the story.

Now you've created your own hilarious MAD LIBS® game!

JOURNAL ENTRY: BILL CIPHER

ADJECTIVE _____

NOUN _____

ADJECTIVE _____

PART OF THE BODY _____

A PLACE _____

PERSON IN ROOM _____

VERB ENDING IN "ING" _____

EXCLAMATION _____

NOUN _____

ADJECTIVE _____

NOUN _____

TYPE OF FOOD _____

VERB _____

ANIMAL (PLURAL) _____

NOUN _____

MAD LIBS®

JOURNAL ENTRY: BILL CIPHER

Hey, it's Dipper. Have you seen this really _____ entry in the
ADJECTIVE

journal about a/an _____ called Bill Cipher? The author
NOUN

writes that he's "the most powerful and _____ creature" he's
ADJECTIVE

ever encountered and to never let him into your _____!
PART OF THE BODY

I know Gideon wanted (the) _____ for himself, but getting
A PLACE

_____ to enter Grunkle Stan's mind was totally
PERSON IN ROOM

_____ too far! _____! At least the author
VERB ENDING IN "ING"   EXCLAMATION

had discovered a/an _____ that allowed me, Mabel, and
NOUN

Soos to dive into Stan's mind and go after Bill. Entering someone else's

mindscape sure is _____, especially if that mindscape
ADJECTIVE

belongs to my _____. But it turns out taking down a triangle
NOUN

demon guy can be a piece of _____, especially when I
TYPE OF FOOD

have laser vision and can _____, and Mabel has
VERB

_____ for fists. Clearly, my sister's got harnessing the
ANIMAL (PLURAL)

power of imagination down to a/an _____.
NOUN

MAD LIBS® is fun to play with friends, but you can also play it by yourself! To begin with, DO NOT look at the story on the page below. Fill in the blanks on this page with the words called for. Then, using the words you have selected, fill in the blank spaces in the story.

Now you've created your own hilarious MAD LIBS® game!

TRUSTING GRUNKLE STAN (?)

VERB _____

PLURAL NOUN _____

ADJECTIVE _____

PLURAL NOUN _____

NOUN _____

ADJECTIVE _____

NOUN _____

PART OF THE BODY (PLURAL) _____

NOUN _____

NOUN _____

PART OF THE BODY (PLURAL) _____

VERB _____

NOUN _____

NOUN _____

MAD LIBS

TRUSTING GRUNKLE STAN (?)

Mabel here. Ever have one of those days where government agents

show up to _____ your grunkle for stealing nuclear
                   VERB

_____? Yeah, me too. And to make matters _____,
PLURAL NOUN   ADJECTIVE

Dipper and I found a box full of Grunkle Stan's IDs with fake

_____ on them. Maybe Stan really was leading an evil
PLURAL NOUN

double life . . . maybe he wasn't even my real _____. We
                                                    NOUN

learned the truth when gravity literally fell because of a/an

_____ portal-thingie, and I floated up into the air like a
ADJECTIVE

_____! Grunkle Stan asked me to look into his
NOUN

_____ and decide if I really thought he was a bad
PART OF THE BODY (PLURAL)

_____. I decided to take a/an _____ of faith! I
NOUN   NOUN

threw my _____ in the air and let myself
              PART OF THE BODY (PLURAL)

_____ up and away. And at the end of the _____,
VERB   NOUN

the only thing not up in the _____ was my trust for Grunkle
                                  NOUN

Stan!

MAD LIBS® is fun to play with friends, but you can also play it by yourself! To begin with, DO NOT look at the story on the page below. Fill in the blanks on this page with the words called for. Then, using the words you have selected, fill in the blank spaces in the story.

Now you've created your own hilarious MAD LIBS® game!

THE AUTHOR OF THE JOURNALS

EXCLAMATION _____

ADJECTIVE _____

NOUN _____

VERB ENDING IN "ING" _____

PERSON IN ROOM _____

PLURAL NOUN _____

PART OF THE BODY _____

CELEBRITY _____

PLURAL NOUN _____

ADVERB _____

NUMBER _____

NOUN _____

PLURAL NOUN _____

ADJECTIVE _____

ADJECTIVE _____

VERB _____

NOUN _____

MAD LIBS®
THE AUTHOR
OF THE JOURNALS

_____, it's Dipper! Oh man, oh man, this is _____!
  EXCLAMATION   ADJECTIVE

The biggest mystery of the _____ has been solved! I can't
                                       NOUN

stop _____! *Aaaaaahhhh!* Ahem, okay, okay, let me
        VERB ENDING IN "ING"

explain. When Mabel left Grunkle _____'s portal on, I
                                PERSON IN ROOM

thought we were all _____. A bright light flashed from the
                     PLURAL NOUN

_____ of the portal, and me, Stan, _____,
  PART OF THE BODY   CELEBRITY

and Mabel were suspended in the air like _____.
                                   PLURAL NOUN

_____, a dark figure emerged. He picked up the journal
  ADVERB

from the ground with his _____-fingered hand—just like
                      NUMBER

the one on the _____'s cover! That's when Stan confirmed
               NOUN

that this was the author of the journal's _____. Not only
                            PLURAL NOUN

that, he was Stan's twin brother! I mean, how _____ is that?
                                ADJECTIVE

Oh man, I'm so _____, I think I'm gonna _____.
           ADJECTIVE   VERB

Does anyone have a bucket . . . or a/an _____?
                                  NOUN

MAD LIBS® is fun to play with friends, but you can also play it by yourself! To begin with, DO NOT look at the story on the page below. Fill in the blanks on this page with the words called for. Then, using the words you have selected, fill in the blank spaces in the story.

Now you've created your own hilarious MAD LIBS® game!

KINGS OF NEW JERSEY

PLURAL NOUN _____

PLURAL NOUN _____

ARTICLE OF CLOTHING (PLURAL) _____

PART OF THE BODY _____

ADJECTIVE _____

ADJECTIVE _____

NOUN _____

NOUN _____

A PLACE _____

PLURAL NOUN _____

NOUN _____

PLURAL NOUN _____

VERB _____

ADJECTIVE _____

NUMBER _____

ADJECTIVE _____

MAD LIBS

KINGS OF NEW JERSEY

Back in 1960-something, two twin _____ were gallivanting

PLURAL NOUN

through childhood as the best of _____. Stanford Pines, an

PLURAL NOUN

exceptionally smart, _____-wearing kid with six

ARTICLE OF CLOTHING (PLURAL)

fingers on each _____, was fascinated with investigating

PART OF THE BODY

the _____-natural. His _____ twin brother,

ADJECTIVE ... ADJECTIVE

Stanley Pines, didn't care so much for research, but adventure was

right up his _____. One day, they stumbled upon an old

NOUN

_____ in a cove and both realized their mutual dream of

NOUN

sailing to (the) _____. Declaring themselves "_____

A PLACE ... PLURAL NOUN

of New Jersey," the boys vowed to fix up the vessel and dubbed her the

Stan o' _____. But as the _____ went by, Stanley

NOUN ... PLURAL NOUN

and Stanford started to _____ apart. Little did the brothers

VERB

know that a/an _____ event _____ years down

ADJECTIVE ... NUMBER

the line would reunite them in Gravity Falls, Oregon—if only for a/an

_____ time.

ADJECTIVE

MAD LIBS® is fun to play with friends, but you can also play it by yourself! To begin with, DO NOT look at the story on the page below. Fill in the blanks on this page with the words called for. Then, using the words you have selected, fill in the blank spaces in the story.

Now you've created your own hilarious MAD LIBS® game!

THE GENIUS AND THE GRIFTER

VERB (PAST TENSE) _____

A PLACE _____

NOUN _____

PERSON IN ROOM _____

VERB ENDING IN "S" _____

ADJECTIVE _____

PLURAL NOUN _____

TYPE OF FOOD (PLURAL) _____

PLURAL NOUN _____

NOUN _____

PLURAL NOUN _____

EXCLAMATION _____

NOUN _____

PART OF THE BODY _____

COLOR _____

NOUN _____

NOUN _____

MAD LIBS
THE GENIUS AND THE GRIFTER

After getting _____ out of (the) _____ by
               VERB (PAST TENSE)   A PLACE

his father, young Stanley Pines hit the _____ as a vagabond.
                                              NOUN

Meanwhile, his twin brother, _____, moved to Gravity
                              PERSON IN ROOM

_____, a town with a/an _____ concentration of
VERB ENDING IN "S"   ADJECTIVE

strange _____, to conduct research. After encounters with
        PLURAL NOUN

the likes of gnomes, uni-_____, and spooky
                         TYPE OF FOOD (PLURAL)

_____, Ford had a dream about a triangular _____
PLURAL NOUN   NOUN

that wanted to help him uncover the _____ of the universe.
                                     PLURAL NOUN

_____, it was Bill! Just when it was almost too late, the two
EXCLAMATION

brothers reunited in Gravity Falls. But a/an _____ broke
                                                  NOUN

out between them, leaving Stan with a burn scar on his _____
                                                        PART OF THE BODY

and Stanford vanishing into a portal in a flash of _____! For
                                                     COLOR

years, Stan tried in vain to fix the _____. But it wasn't until
                                        NOUN

Dipper and Mabel came along that he finally figured out how to turn

the _____ back on and bring his brother back!
      NOUN

MAD LIBS® is fun to play with friends, but you can also play it by yourself! To begin with, DO NOT look at the story on the page below. Fill in the blanks on this page with the words called for. Then, using the words you have selected, fill in the blank spaces in the story.

Now you've created your own hilarious MAD LIBS® game!

TWINS RUN IN THE FAMILY

ADJECTIVE _____

PLURAL NOUN _____

ADJECTIVE _____

NUMBER _____

PLURAL NOUN _____

NOUN _____

ANIMAL _____

TYPE OF FOOD (PLURAL) _____

OCCUPATION _____

ADVERB _____

PLURAL NOUN _____

NOUN _____

PERSON IN ROOM _____

NOUN _____

OCCUPATION _____

PLURAL NOUN _____

ADJECTIVE _____

MAD LIBS

TWINS RUN IN THE FAMILY

It turns out both _____ and fraternal _____ run
                    ADJECTIVE   PLURAL NOUN

in the Pines family! With the reveal of Great-Uncle Ford as Stan's

_____ brother, Dipper and Mabel now have _____
   ADJECTIVE   NUMBER

_____ for the price of one! Let's find out which
  PLURAL NOUN

_____ takes after who!
     NOUN

Stan and Mabel:

_____-*tective* is their favorite TV show! On any given
    ANIMAL

evening, you'll find Stan and Mabel snacking on _____
                                              TYPE OF FOOD (PLURAL)

and cheering on a certain feathered _____. They love to
                                        OCCUPATION

poke fun at Dipper, _____, of course. Especially if the joke
                        ADVERB

involves solving _____ and kissing a/an _____
                   PLURAL NOUN   NOUN

with Wendy's face on it.

Ford and _____:
            PERSON IN ROOM

Ford and Dipper are both _____ smart and journal obsessed.
                              NOUN

Ford even invited Dipper to become his _____! Ever hear of
                                          OCCUPATION

Dungeons, _____, *& More Dungeons*? It's their
               PLURAL NOUN

_____ game—in any dimension!
   ADJECTIVE

MAD LIBS® is fun to play with friends, but you can also play it by yourself! To begin with, DO NOT look at the story on the page below. Fill in the blanks on this page with the words called for. Then, using the words you have selected, fill in the blank spaces in the story.

Now you've created your own hilarious MAD LIBS® game!

MABEL'S GUIDE TO SURVIVING THE APOCALYPSE!

VERB _____

LETTER OF THE ALPHABET _____

NOUN _____

VERB _____

NOUN _____

NOUN _____

ANIMAL (PLURAL) _____

ADJECTIVE _____

NOUN _____

ADJECTIVE _____

TYPE OF FOOD (PLURAL) _____

VERB ENDING IN "ING" _____

PLURAL NOUN _____

VEHICLE _____

ADJECTIVE _____

SILLY WORD _____

MAD LIBS®
MABEL'S GUIDE
TO SURVIVING THE
APOCALYPSE!

Give me an M—*M!* _____ me a/an _____—
_____ VERB _____ LETTER OF THE ALPHABET

VERB — LETTER OF THE ALPHABET

Ah, you get the _____—it's Mabel again! This time with a
NOUN

guide to the apocalypse. Let's _____, shall we?
VERB

1. If a triangular _____ demon uses Weirdmageddon to trap
NOUN

you inside of a fantastical _____ of your own imagination,
NOUN

make the best of it with _____ that serve you snacks,
ANIMAL (PLURAL)

and a soundtrack of _____ dance music!
ADJECTIVE

2. If your imagination imprisons you in an enchanted _____,
NOUN

dream up some _____ castle guards—like
ADJECTIVE

_____ with big arms!
TYPE OF FOOD (PLURAL)

3. Let my guide on _____ inspire you! Dream up
VERB ENDING IN "ING"

some cute _____ to drive you around in a convertible
PLURAL NOUN

_____ and say _____ things to you, like
VEHICLE ADJECTIVE

_____!
SILLY WORD

MAD LIBS® is fun to play with friends, but you can also play it by yourself! To begin with, DO NOT look at the story on the page below. Fill in the blanks on this page with the words called for. Then, using the words you have selected, fill in the blank spaces in the story.

Now you've created your own hilarious MAD LIBS® game!

THE MYSTERY SHACK ATTACKS!

NOUN _____

ANIMAL _____

NOUN _____

PART OF THE BODY _____

SILLY WORD _____

ANIMAL _____

NOUN _____

ADJECTIVE _____

PLURAL NOUN _____

NOUN _____

NOUN _____

ADJECTIVE _____

PART OF THE BODY _____

TYPE OF FOOD _____

PLURAL NOUN _____

NOUN _____

ADJECTIVE _____

ANIMAL _____

MAD LIBS®
THE MYSTERY SHACK ATTACKS!

Dudes! Remember me? Soos? The _____ from the Mystery
NOUN

Shack who kinda looks like a hairless _____? Oh man, you
ANIMAL

missed out on the Mystery _____ kicking some major
NOUN

_____ during Weirdma-_____! That old
PART OF THE BODY   SILLY WORD

McGucket guy (the one married to a/an _____) said
ANIMAL

he had blueprints to turn the Shack into a giant, fighting

mech-_____. That's _____, right? While I
NOUN   ADJECTIVE

introduced McGucket to a few anime _____ for inspiration,
PLURAL NOUN

Dipper and Mabel led a bunch of _____ Falls citizens who
NOUN

renovated the place into the Shack-Tron. Dudes, this _____
NOUN

had everything: _____, stomping, mechanical legs and even
ADJECTIVE

a/an _____ made out of a live dinosaur! _____
PART OF THE BODY   TYPE OF FOOD

and Grenda were in charge of the controls, while Waddles got to fire at

some interdimensional _____ using a cannon made out of
PLURAL NOUN

the totem _____ from the _____ yard! Boy, it's
NOUN   ADJECTIVE

times like that I wish I was a/an _____!
ANIMAL

MAD LIBS® is fun to play with friends, but you can also play it by yourself! To begin with, DO NOT look at the story on the page below. Fill in the blanks on this page with the words called for. Then, using the words you have selected, fill in the blank spaces in the story.

Now you've created your own hilarious MAD LIBS® game!

AN ENDING TO (HOPEFULLY) REMEMBER

ADJECTIVE _____

NOUN _____

PLURAL NOUN _____

ADJECTIVE _____

PLURAL NOUN _____

SILLY WORD _____

CELEBRITY _____

NOUN _____

NOUN _____

NOUN _____

EXCLAMATION _____

NOUN _____

NOUN _____

ADJECTIVE _____

ANIMAL _____

MAD LIBS
AN ENDING TO
(HOPEFULLY) REMEMBER

Anyone from Gravity Falls could tell you that _____-mageddon
                                              ADJECTIVE

ended with a/an _____. When Bill told the grunkles that he
                 NOUN

would kill the _____ if Ford didn't fork over some
               PLURAL NOUN

_____ information, Stan and Ford swapped _____
 ADJECTIVE   PLURAL NOUN

and tricked Bill with an old switch-a-_____ scheme. Stan,
                                       SILLY WORD

dressed like _____, agreed to tell Bill what he wanted to
             CELEBRITY

know. But, when Bill entered Stan's _____, he was shocked
                                     NOUN

to realize he was in the wrong _____! Then, with a blast of
                                NOUN

his memory-erasing _____, Ford erased Stan's mind,
                    NOUN

destroyed Bill, and Weirdmageddon was over! _____!
                                             EXCLAMATION

But this left Stan with no memory! Determined to save her grunkle,

Mabel counted on her trusty _____ to remind Stan of their
                             NOUN

summer together in Gravity Falls. In the end, it was Waddles who

rekindled Stan's _____. After all, how could Stan forget how
                  NOUN

_____ that _____ was?
 ADJECTIVE   ANIMAL

MAD LIBS® is fun to play with friends, but you can also play it by yourself! To begin with, DO NOT look at the story on the page below. Fill in the blanks on this page with the words called for. Then, using the words you have selected, fill in the blank spaces in the story.

Now you've created your own hilarious MAD LIBS® game!

GOODBYE, GRAVITY FALLS

ADJECTIVE _____

ADJECTIVE _____

PLURAL NOUN _____

NUMBER _____

NOUN _____

NOUN _____

VERB _____

NOUN _____

SILLY WORD _____

NOUN _____

PLURAL NOUN _____

ARTICLE OF CLOTHING _____

ADJECTIVE _____

EXCLAMATION _____

VEHICLE _____

PART OF THE BODY (PLURAL) _____

A PLACE _____

VERB ENDING IN "S" _____

GOODBYE, GRAVITY FALLS

Dipper: Our summer in Gravity Falls was _____.
ADJECTIVE

We ventured into the _____ outdoors, solved countless
ADJECTIVE

_____ . . .
PLURAL NOUN

Mabel: And we turned _____ years old!
NUMBER

Dipper: Yeah! The whole _____ came together and threw us a
NOUN

birthday _____! Even Gideon showed up. Seems like he's
NOUN

trying to _____ over a new _____.
VERB   NOUN

Mabel: _____, I'm still not gonna date him. Anyway, my
SILLY WORD

favorite end-of-_____ moment was when we got to watch as
NOUN

Soos's _____ came true. Stan crowned him with his almighty
PLURAL NOUN

_____ and dubbed Soos the new Mr. Mystery!
ARTICLE OF CLOTHING

Dipper: I think the _____ part was saying _____
ADJECTIVE   EXCLAMATION

to Grunkle Stan at the _____ stop. We all had tears in our
VEHICLE

_____, but there's always next summer. And if you're
PART OF THE BODY (PLURAL)

ever traveling through (the) _____, look out for a sign that
A PLACE

says Gravity _____!
VERB ENDING IN "S"